I Am A Big Brother
Kuv Yog Ib Tug Tij Laug

written by:
Tory Envy

illustrated by:
Agia Putri
Qaharu Aulia

Copyright © 2022 by Tory Envy
All rights reserved.

All rights reserved. No part of this book may be reproduced or transmitted in any form by any means, electronic or mechanical, including photocopying, recording, or by any information or retrieval systems, without the written permission of the publisher.

ISBN Hardback: 978-8-955702-1-2
ISBN Paperback: 979-8-9855702-0-5

First Edition 2022.
Illustrations by Agia Putri & Kaharu Aulia
Edited by Yia Lee
Published by Story Cloth Co

This book belongs to
Phau ntawv no yog
_____ li.

Baby arrived today.

Me ab los txog hnub no.

I am a big brother.

Kuv yog ib tug tij laug.

Watch me help
take care of baby.

Saib kuv pab zov me ab.

Baby cries very loud.

Me ab quaj nrov heev.

It's time to change
baby's diaper.

Txog sijhawm hloov me
ab daim pawm lawm.

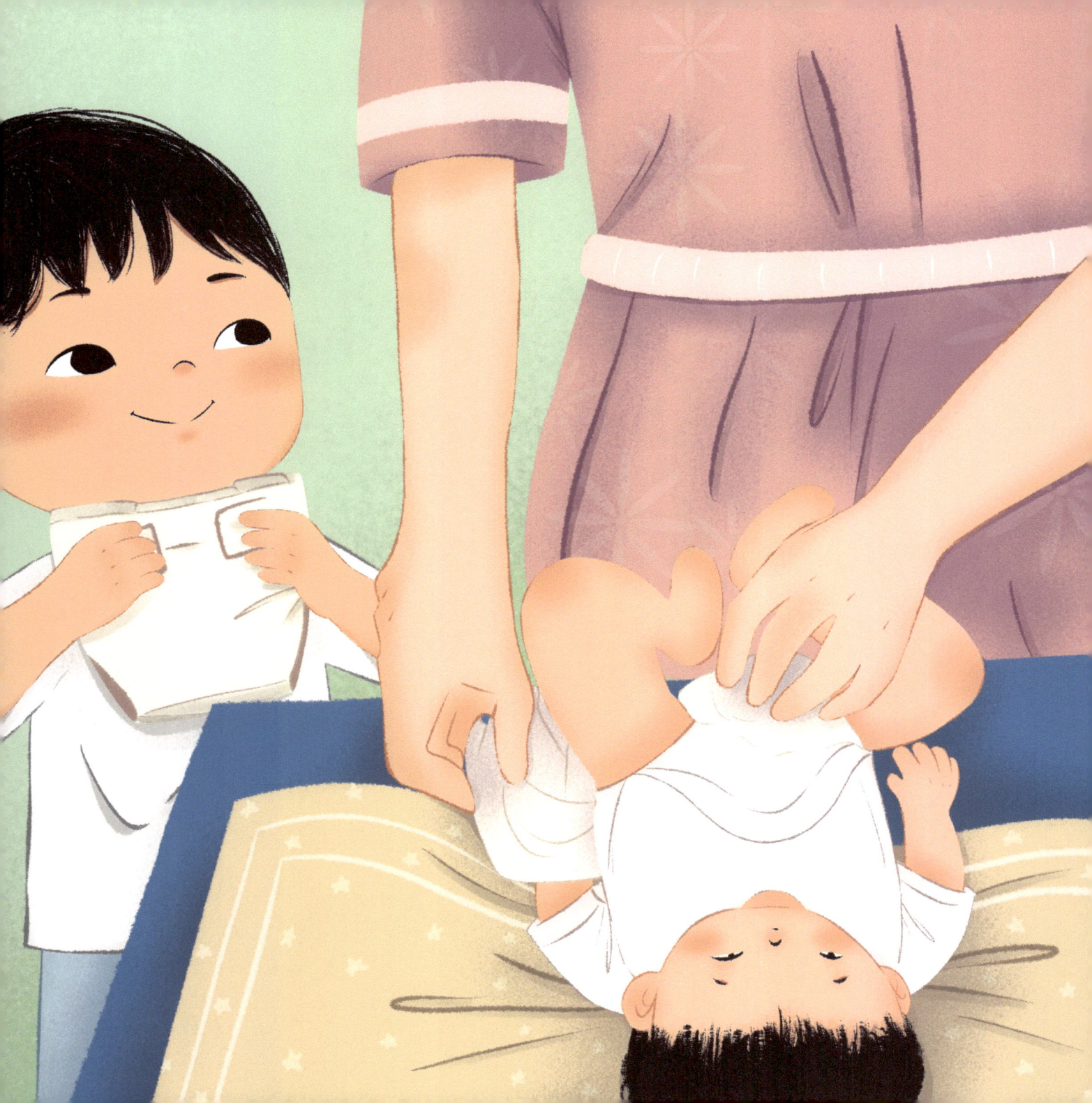

Baby likes it when
I share my toys.

Me ab nyiam thaum
kuv cia nws ua si nrog
kuv cov khoom.

I can teach baby many things.

Kuv txawj qhia me ab ntau yam.

Baby is very messy.

Me ab ua sw heev.

Its bath time!

Txog sijhawm mus da dej lawm!

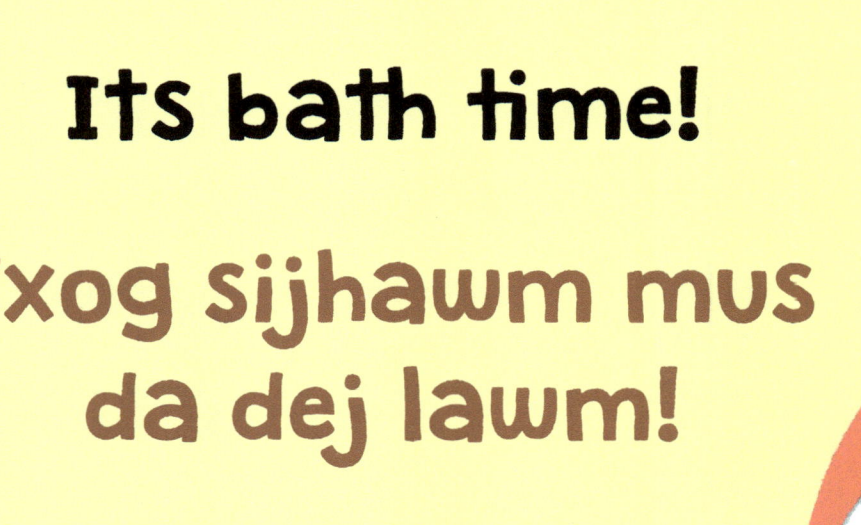

Be quiet when baby is sleeping.

Nyob ntsiag to thaum me ab pw tsaug zog.

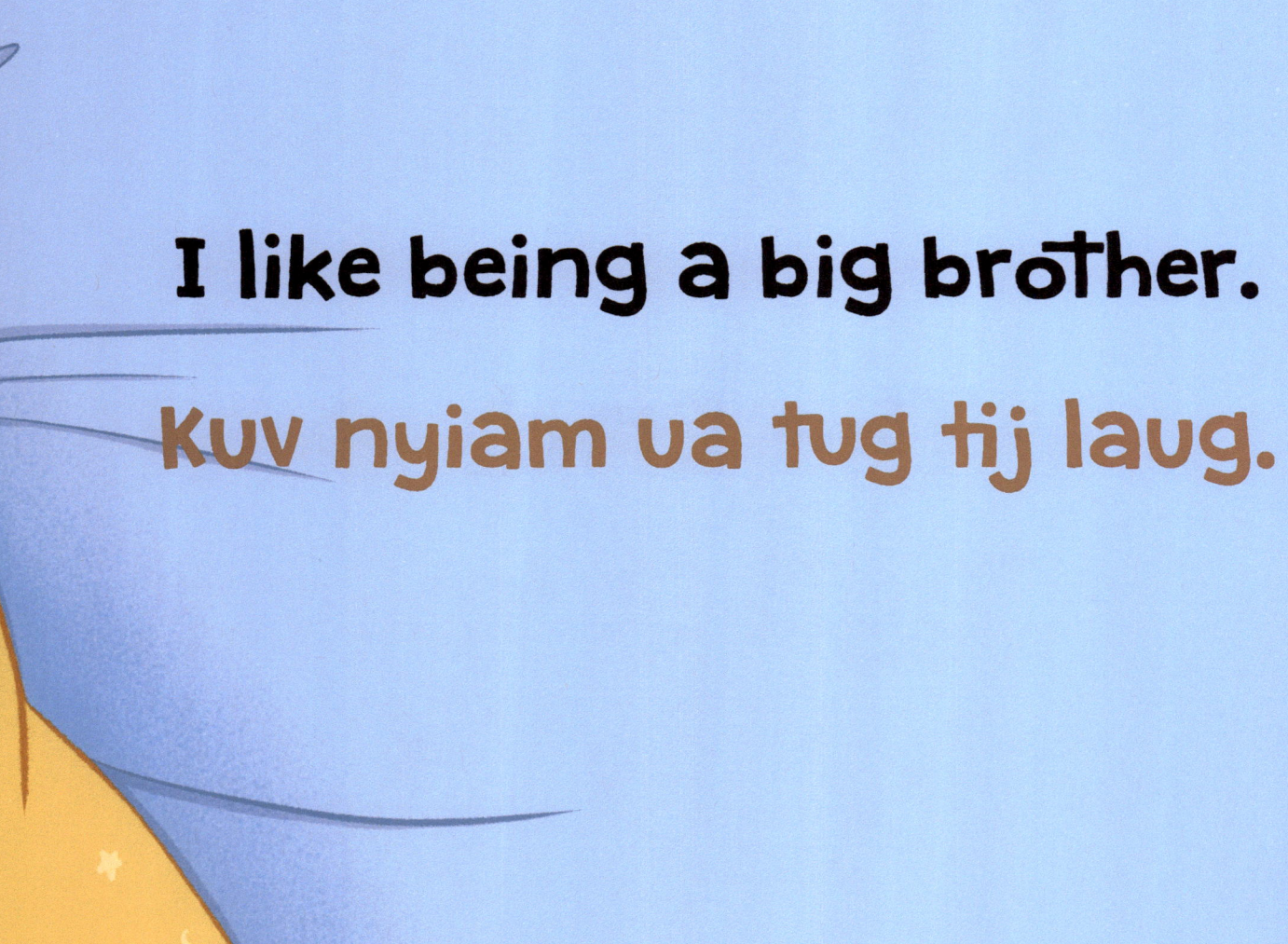

I like being a big brother.

Kuv nyiam ua tug tij laug.

The End.
Tag Lawm.

www.ingramcontent.com/pod-product-compliance
Lightning Source LLC
Chambersburg PA
CBHW040724060526
44119CB00083B/314